Bringing Big Emotions to a Bigger God

GOD, I feeL SAD

written by
Michelle Nietert, LPC-S
Tama Fortner

illustrated by
Nomar Perez

For the One who fills my life with Joy.
—TF

To the previous and current Community Counseling Associates
staff members. Thanks for allowing God to use you as His vessels
of love and hope to kids and their families for decades.
—MN

To my wife and kids, who are God's amazing handiwork.
—NP

ZONDERKIDZ

God, I Feel Sad
Copyright © 2023 by Michelle Nietert and Tama Fortner
Illustrations © 2023 by Zondervan

Requests for information should be addressed to:

Zonderkidz, 3900 Sparks Drive, Grand Rapids, Michigan 49546

Hardcover ISBN 978-0-310-14084-9
Audio download ISBN 978-0-310-14088-7
Ebook ISBN 978-0-310-14087-0

Tama Fortner is represented by Cyle Young of Cyle Young Literary Elite, LLC. Michelle Nietert is represented by
the literary agency of The Blythe Daniel Agency, Inc., P.O. Box 64197, Colorado Springs, CO 80962.

Zonderkidz is a trademark of Zondervan.

Zondervan titles may be purchased in bulk for educational, business, fundraising, or sales promotional use.
For information, please email SpecialMarkets@Zondervan.com.

Zonderkidz is a trademark of Zondervan.

Illustrations: Nomar Perez
Editors: Katherine Jacobs/Jacque Alberta
Design and art direction: Cindy Davis

Printed in India

23 24 25 26 27 28 / REP / 21 20 19 18 17 16 15 14 13 12 11 10 9 8 7 6 5 4 3 2 1

When God made you, He gave you emotions.

Some emotions feel wonderful, like happy, excited, and surprised.
But others aren't as fun to feel, like scared, and mad, and ...

sad.

Sad can happen when you fall and skin your knee or when someone hurts your feelings. It can creep in when you're feeling lonely and left out.

Or it can *crash* in when a friend won't play with you or you aren't picked to be on the team.

A little sad can sneak in when you don't feel well or when someone you care about is sick. And sad can get *really* big if someone close to you dies.

You might even feel sad simply because you see someone else feeling unhappy and blue.

Sad isn't the most fun emotion to feel,
but there's a reason you're sad sometimes.

It's God's way of helping you know that you've been hurt—in your body or in your heart. And it lets you know something isn't quite right with your world.

Sad looks different on each person's face.

It might pull your eyebrows up high and make your eyes droop down.

It can turn your smile into a frown.

And it spills out in words like ...

My heart hurts.

It's not fair.

I want it back.

I messed up.

It's all my fault.

Sad can make you feel tired and heavy and as slow as a sloth. You might want to whimper like a puppy who needs comfort and extra hugs.

Or maybe you'd rather spend the day snuggled up with someone you love.

A listening ear could be just the thing you need.

Or you might simply want to be left alone to think.

When you're sad, how can you begin to feel better again?
First, give your feeling a name. Say, "I feel sad" … or upset …
or disappointed. Pick the word that best fits you.

Next, figure out where your body is feeling the sad. Is it tight in your throat or heavy on your shoulders? Is it aching in your tummy or tightening up your chest?

Or is your sad slipping out in tears?

It's okay to *feel* your feelings. Don't pretend they're not there.
Let the sad out so you can start to feel better again. Sigh a big sigh
or have a good cry. Think about things that make you smile.

Draw a picture, sing a song, or write all about your feelings in a story. Get up and move to your favorite music. Dance until the sadness disappears.

Talk to a grown-up. Talk to a friend. Tell someone who cares about you.

Most of all, talk to God. He knows just how you feel, and He's always there to listen and help you.

Some sadness goes away quickly. Some sadness sticks around. And some sadness comes and goes like the waves at the edge of the ocean.

Tiny waves roll in—just big enough to wet your toes—and you feel a little blue. But those little waves quickly roll out and you start to feel better again.

Other waves are big and huge. They swirl around and soak you with sad all the way through. It might take a little longer, but those big waves will roll back out too.

Yes, sadness happens for a reason. But God doesn't want you to feel sad forever. That's why He offers you hope too. *Hope* is God's promise to help you find your happy again.

Every day, and in so many ways, God sends you messages of hope. One might be a rainbow on a day that's gray and rainy.

Another could be a hug from a friend, a silly sight that makes you giggle, or a flower blooming in a sidewalk crack. With each message of hope, God is saying, "I'm here with you, and it's going to be okay."

How many of God's messages can you find? Ask Him to open your eyes and help you see them. Can you find one, or two, or three hundred thirty-four?

Because God's love and goodness are everywhere and all around you … even when you're feeling sad.

The LORD is close to the brokenhearted.
—Psalm 34:18

Dear Parent,

It's important for children to experience all their feelings—even the hard ones. When you recognize that your child is feeling sad, encourage them to name their emotions and talk about them. Let them know it's okay to feel this way. Give them opportunities to express and release their feelings—through tears, drawing, writing, or dancing. Do this even for the little sadnesses of life. (Yes, even the ones that don't seem important to you.) Children will need at least ninety seconds to recognize and process their emotions in order to move past them.

There are times, though, when sadness can grow so huge and heavy that it seems to be the only thing in your child's world. That's when it's time to teach your child to put their sadness away. Talk them through these steps:

- Imagine gathering up all the sadness in your arms. Let's pack it away in this invisible box. Don't let any sneak out! Close the lid tight.
- Now, think of something that makes you smile. Do something fun. Hug someone you love. Run and play with your friends. Let yourself be happy.
- Then, when you need to—and your heart will tell you when—take the sadness out of the box. Let yourself feel it again, just for a little while. Talk, write, or draw it out. Then take a deep breath and pack that sadness back into the box. Guess what? It won't be as big as it was before!
- Every time you take the sadness out, it will be a little smaller and a little smaller … until, one day, you won't need the box anymore.

By helping your child process their emotions, you are encouraging them to develop skills they'll use their entire lives. For more information and ideas on helping children cope with emotions, please visit www.GodIFeel.com.